WHY WAS MARY
EMBARRASSED?

Six days before the Passover, Jesus arrived at Bethany, where Lazarus lived, whom Jesus had raised from the dead. Here a dinner was given in Jesus' honour. Martha served, while Lazarus was among those reclining at the table with him. Then Mary took about a pint of pure nard, an expensive perfume; she poured it on Jesus' feet and wiped his feet with her hair. And the house was filled with the fragrance of the perfume.

But one of his disciples, Judas Iscariot, who was later to betray him, objected, "Why wasn't this perfume sold and the money given to the poor? It was worth a year's wages." He did not say this because he cared about the poor but because he was a thief; as keeper of the money bag, he used to help himself to what was put into it.

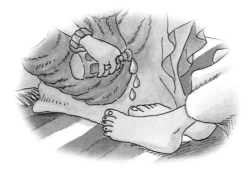

"Leave her alone," Jesus replied. "It was intended that she should save this perfume for the day of my burial. You will always have the poor among you, but you will not always have me."

John 12: 1-8, NIV

Why Was Mary Embarrassed?

Scandinavia Publishing House
Drejervej 15,3 DK-Copenhagen NV Denmark
Tel. (+45) 3531 0330
www.scanpublishing.dk
info@scanpublishing.dk

Design by Ben Alex
Produced by Scandinavia Publishing House

Printed in China
ISBN: 9788772470368

WHY WAS MARY EMBARRASSED?

By Pauline Youd
Illustrated by Elaine Garvin

SCANDINAVIA

Mary took a beautiful bottle down from the shelf. Holding it with both hands, she turned it around and around in the candlelight. She lifted the lid. The sweet smell of perfume filled the room.

Mary quickly put the cover back on the bottle. She looked across the hallway to the living room. Dinner was over. Jesus was sitting with his disciples around the low table talking to Mary's brother, Lazarus.

7

Jesus was a very special friend of their family. He had taught them about God's love.

Jesus had made Mary's brother, Lazarus, alive and well. Mary was very grateful to Jesus. She wanted to do something special for him.

Suddenly Mary had an idea. She clutched the bottle and walked into the room where the men sat talking. Kneeling beside Jesus, Mary lifted the lid and poured the perfume on Jesus' feet. Then she wiped his feet with her hair.

One of the men jumped up and cried, "What a waste! Why didn't you sell that perfume and give the money to the poor?"

Mary was very embarrassed. Her face turned red. She wanted to run out of the room.

Then she felt Jesus' gentle hand on her shoulder. "Leave her alone, Judas," Jesus said to the man. "She gave me this gift because she loves me. What she has done for me will be remembered and talked about for thousands of years."

Do you like to give gifts? Almost everyone does. Most of the time we try to give what we think the other person really wants. But how do you feel when someone laughs at your gift or acts like he or she doesn't want it?

Mary gave Jesus the most precious thing she had. She gave it because she loved him. Jesus was happy to accept Mary's gift.

The most precious thing you can give Jesus is your love. Jesus said, "If you really love me, you will obey my teaching." Have you ever thought of your obedience as a gift to Jesus? It's a gift only you can give him.

13

"Leave her alone," Jesus
replied. *"It was intended that
she should save this perfume
for the day of my burial. You
will always have the poor
among you, but you will not
always have me."*

John 12:7-8

WONDER BOOKS
Lessons to learn from 12 Bible characters

God's Love

Self-giving

Prayer Overcomes Fear

Praising God

Prayer Obtains Wisdom

Listening to God

Trust

Perseverance

Loving Obedience

Persistence

Asking Advice

Trusting God's plan